10/11

Count Your Way through

South Africa

by **Jim Haskins** and **Kathleen Benson**

illustrations by **Alissa Neibert**

Ⓜ Millbrook Press / Minneapolis

To Negasi, Tessema, and Zauditu Haskins —K.B.
To my parents and Mike —A.N.

The authors gratefully acknowledge the help of Agnes Tsele-Maselonyane, Trade Division, Consulate General of South Africa, New York City.

Millbrook Press, Inc.
A division of Lerner Publishing Group
241 First Avenue North
Minneapolis, MN 55401 U.S.A.

Website address: www.lernerbooks.com

Library of Congress Cataloging-in-Publication Data

Haskins, James, 1941–
    Count your way through South Africa / by Jim Haskins and Kathleen Benson ; illustrations by Alissa Neibert.
    p.   cm. — (Count your way)
    ISBN-13: 978–1–57505–883–2 (lib. bdg. : alk. paper)
    ISBN-10: 1–57505–883–9 (lib. bdg. : alk. paper)
    1. South Africa—Juvenile literature. 2. Zulu language—Numerals—Juvenile literature. 3. Counting—Juvenile literature.
I. Benson, Kathleen. II. Neibert, Alissa, ill. III. Title.
DT1719.H37 2007
968—dc22   2005032537

Manufactured in the United States of America
1 2 3 4 5 6 – DP – 12 11 10 09 08 07

Introduction

On the southern tip of Africa lies the country of South Africa. More than 47 million people live there. South Africa has an area of 471,445 square miles. That is about the same size as the states of California, Nevada, Utah, and Arizona combined.

South Africa has 11 official languages. Two of them are English and Afrikaans. Afrikaans is a mix of Dutch and other languages. (Dutch people began settling in South Africa in the 1600s.) The other nine official languages are African. Many black South Africans speak Zulu. We will count through South Africa in this language.

kunye

(KOO-nyeh)

One gold nugget like this is the key to much of South Africa's history. Large amounts of gold were discovered there in 1886. Gold mining brought more British and other European people to the area. They forced many native Africans to work in the mines. Europeans also brought in workers from other parts of the world.

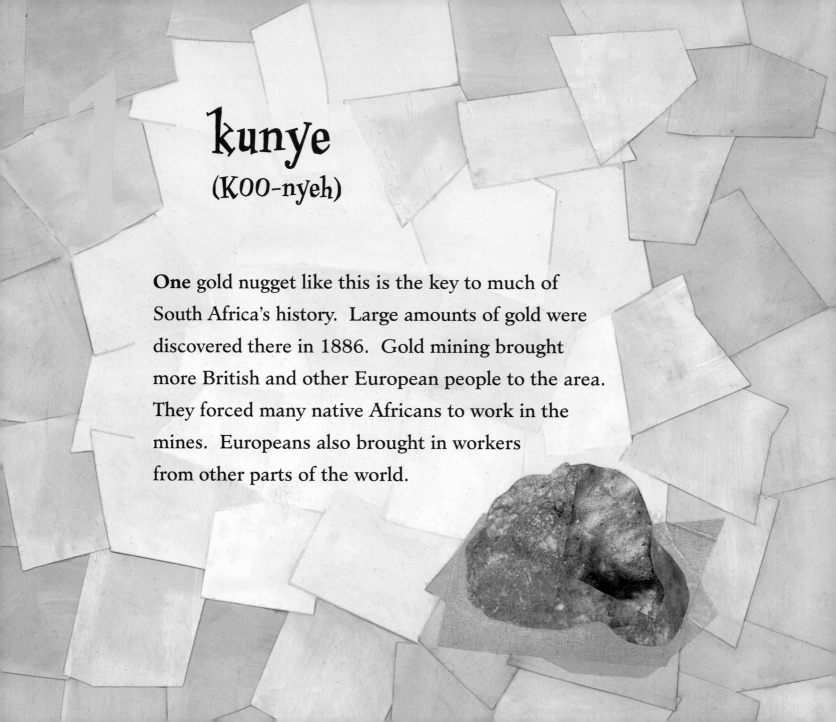

kubili
(koo-BEE-lee)

A group of **two**-horned springboks gathers in the Kalahari Desert. These beautiful animals can spring, or pronk, high into the air when they get excited. Some springboks can pronk 12 feet. That is higher than the ceilings in most houses! The springbok is South Africa's national animal.

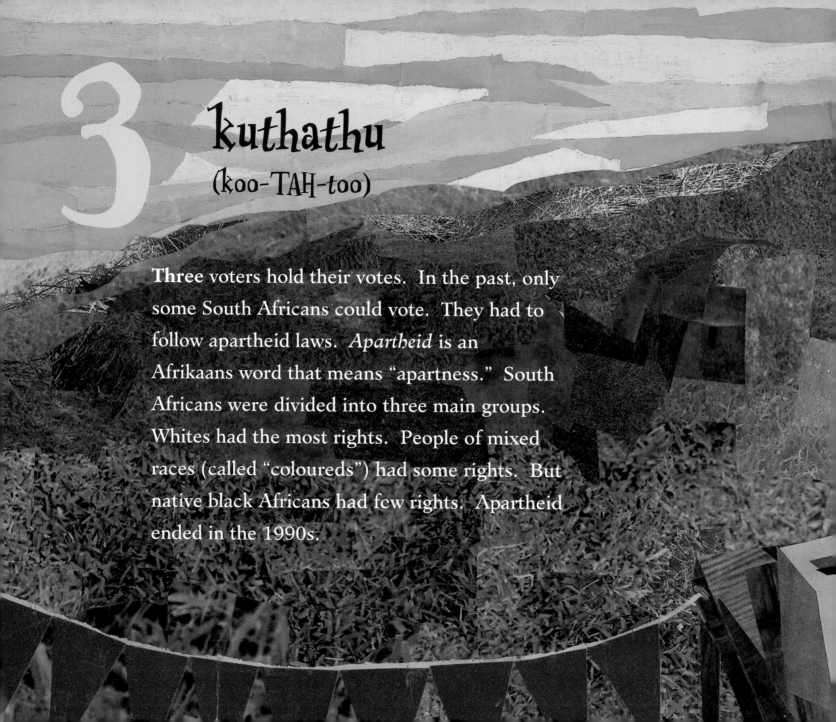

3 kuthathu
(koo-TAH-too)

Three voters hold their votes. In the past, only some South Africans could vote. They had to follow apartheid laws. *Apartheid* is an Afrikaans word that means "apartness." South Africans were divided into three main groups. Whites had the most rights. People of mixed races (called "coloureds") had some rights. But native black Africans had few rights. Apartheid ended in the 1990s.

4 kune

(KOO-neh)

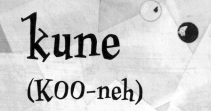

Four traditional crafts in South Africa are basket weaving, pottery, wood carving, and beading. Zulu women have a language of beading. The colors of the beads have different meanings. For example, green can mean happiness or sickness. The women select certain colors and weave them into messages of love, sadness, or jealousy.

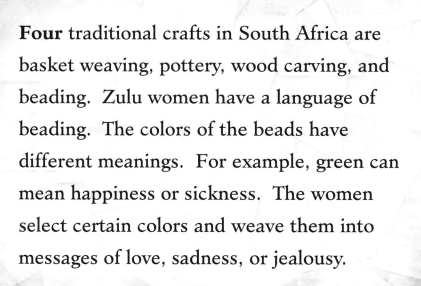

5 kuhlanu
(koo-HLAH-noo)

Five countries border South Africa. Namibia, Botswana, and Zimbabwe lie to the north. Mozambique and Swaziland lie to the east. Inside South Africa is the small Kingdom of Lesotho. The southern part of South Africa ends in the waters of the Atlantic and Indian Oceans.

Atlantic Ocean

isithupa
(ee-see-TOO-pah)

The South African flag has **six** colors. The colors red, white, and blue came from the old South African flag used by the Dutch and British governments. Black, green, and gold were used on the flags of black African groups who fought to end apartheid. The sideways Y on the flag shows all South Africans coming together as one country.

7 isikhombisa
(ee-see-kohm-BEE-sah)

Seven South African children walk to school. During apartheid, white children went to their own schools. Black, mixed race, and Asian children went to different schools. Now South African children can go to school together. They start school when they are about seven years old. They learn a lot of the same subjects that you learn. But their classes are taught in many languages, including Zulu, English, and Afrikaans.

8 isishiyagalombili
(ee-see-SHYAH-gah-lohm-BEE-lee)

Eight foods show the many different cultures found in South Africa. Black African meals often have mealie pap, biltong, and yams. Mealie pap is a kind of cornmeal porridge. Biltong is a snack made of spicy dried meat. Afrikaners enjoy grilling sausages called *boerewors* and cooking stews called *potjiekos*. Curry spices from Indonesia flavor meat kebabs and a meatloaf dish called *bobotie*. People from India added dal to South African dishes. Dal is dried peas, beans, or lentils.

mealie pap

9 isishiyagalolunye
(ee-see-SHYAH-gah-loh-LOO-nyeh)

Nine musicians perform a song. They play traditional instruments made of wood, gourds, shells, beads, and animal horns. South Africa is home to many popular styles of African music. One well-known style of Zulu music is sung without musical instruments. The singers lightly dance as they sing.

ishumi
(ee-SHOO-mee)

Ten products can be made from parts of the baobab tree. It can be made into cloth, glue, medicine, paper, soap, necklaces, strings for musical instruments, baskets, rope, and canoes. Its leaves and fruit can be eaten. Some people have even lived in the huge trunks of baobabs! The baobab can live as long as 1,000 years. It is a protected tree in South Africa.

GLUE

SOAP

Pronunciation Guide

1 / kunye / KOO-nyeh

2 / kubili / koo-BEE-lee

3 / kuthathu / koo-TAH-too

4 / kune / KOO-neh

5 / kuhlanu / koo-HLAH-noo

6 / isithupa / ee-see-TOO-pah

7 / isikhombisa / ee-see-kohm-BEE-sah

8 / isishiyagalombili / ee-see-SHYAH-gah-lohm-BEE-lee

9 / isishiyagalolunye / ee-see-SHYAH-gah-loh-LOO-nyeh

10 / ishumi / ee-SHOO-mee